FORGIVEN AF

(Always Faithful)

From Prison to Purpose

By

Shawn Serfass

For permission requests, write to the publisher at:

Shawn Serfass

2909 Turner Warnell Rd suite 151

Arlington, TX 76001

Facebook @shawnserfass

Ig @shawn2ndchance

First published 2026

ISBN: 979-8-89571-402-7

Interior design by Editor Silas

Edited by Editor Silas

Printed in United States

Dedication Page

This book is dedicated to those who feel too far gone.

To those sitting in cells, staring at concrete walls, wondering if life has already passed them by. To those battling addiction, shame, and the weight of every bad decision they have ever made. To those who have been counted out, written off, and labeled by their worst moment.

I was you.

This is for the people who still hear that small voice deep down telling them there is more—more purpose, more life, more redemption—even when everything around them says otherwise.

This is for the second chances that did not make sense. For the grace that showed up when it was not deserved. For the God who never walked away, even when I did.

To every young man searching for direction, every father trying to rebuild, and every person fighting to become something different—this is proof that your story is not over.

You are not disqualified.

You are not forgotten.

You are not beyond forgiveness.

And if God can do it for me, He can do it for you.

Table of Contents

PROLOGUE

It was cold that morning. The kind of Texas cold that isn't snowing but still makes you pull your hoodie tighter around your neck. The sky was gray, and everything felt quiet and ordinary. I had walked up the street to my mother-in-law, Linda's, house to pick up my son. At the time, he wasn't allowed to stay with us full-time. My wife and I had both failed a CPS drug test, and because of that, we didn't have custody the way we should have. I would go get him in the mornings and bring him back down to our house to spend time together. That was our routine.

As I was walking back down the street with him in my arms, I noticed something that didn't quite sit right. Two or three identical Ford F-150s were parked nearby. Same color. Same model. Men sitting inside. One of them had binoculars up to his face. It caught my attention, but I didn't think it had anything to do with me. In my head, I just thought, Man… somebody's screwed. I didn't feel nervous. I didn't feel exposed. I didn't feel watched. I felt naive. I took my son back into the house, which sat right next door to Linda's house. I put up the little baby gate, as I always did, so he wouldn't wander, and we lay on the floor watching cartoons. That was our thing. I would just stretch out on the carpet and let him climb around while some animated show played in the background. It felt like a regular morning. There was no sense that anything was about to happen.

Then the door exploded inward. It wasn't a knock. It wasn't someone trying the handle. The entire door flew open as men flooded inside, yelling, "DEA! Everyone on the ground!" Eight, maybe ten agents. AR-15s drawn. Red dots moving across the walls, and then across me. And across my son. Time didn't slow down as it does in movies. It sped up. My brain couldn't process it.

I just remember noise. Boots pounding. Men shouting "Clear!" and "Secure!" as they ran into bedrooms and closets. "Who else is here?" "It's just my son and me," I said. My son was screaming. Hysterical. The kind of cry that comes from confusion and terror. And as much as I would love to tell you I stayed calm, I didn't. I started crying too. I had never been in a situation like that. Never had rifles pointed at me.

Never had federal agents tear through my home. Never had my child watch me lose control. They didn't come in cautiously. They came in like they were dismantling a cartel operation. They ripped vents off the walls. Dumped out drawers. Went through every pair of shoes. Every cabinet. Every inch of that apartment. "Where's the drugs?" " Where's the money?" "Where is everything?" By that time, I had already stopped selling. I had stepped away. I wasn't moving anything. I wasn't holding anything. "I don't have anything," I kept telling them. "There's no money. There are no drugs." "What do you have?" "The only thing I have is a Glock in the kitchen drawer."

They found it like they had struck gold. "Got it!" At that point, I wasn't a felon. I was over eighteen. I didn't think I was breaking any law by owning it, but I guess that didn't matter. Linda came running down the street and grabbed my son. She carried him back up the street while he was still crying, and I watched him disappear around the corner. Then they walked me outside. The whole neighborhood was out. Phones up. Recording. Watching. They put me in one of the trucks, one of the same matching F-150s I had noticed just an hour earlier and casually dismissed.

We drove to downtown Fort Worth and pulled into what looked like a bank garage underground, concrete walls, fluorescent lights — but it was the DEA headquarters. As we walked inside, one of the agents leaned toward me and said, "You're going to prison for life. You're never getting out." Life? This was the first time I had ever been in real trouble. I genuinely thought I would get probation. After processing, they transported me to the Tarrant County Jail for the night. The smell hit me before anything else did. The Tarrant County Jail was filthy. Cockroaches are crawling across the floor. Men who hadn't showered in days. The air is thick with sweat and something sour and stale I can't properly describe.

They walked me into a cell. The door shut behind me with a hard metallic clank. And for the first time that entire day, everything went quiet. I sat there and thought, this is actually happening.

This is real. And the question that started forming in my head wasn't about lawyers or bonds or deals. It was this: How did I get here? How did I go from lying on the floor watching cartoons with my son… to sitting in a federal cell in downtown Fort Worth?

That's the story I'm about to tell you.

CHAPTER 1

The Foundation

I was born in Newport, Rhode Island, while my dad was attending the War College. Ours was a Navy family from the start. My father was a career naval officer, a Naval Academy graduate, disciplined, steady, and an amazing leader. He was the kind of man who ironed his own uniforms and conducted himself with the highest integrity. Before I was even a few months old, we moved to Virginia Beach. That's where most of my early childhood lives in my memory—salty air, humid summers, and the constant rhythm of ships coming and going.

My dad would leave for months at a time. Desert Storm. The Gulf War. Deployments that blurred together in my young mind. Six months gone. Sometimes eight. We would stand on the pier waiting for his ship to pull in, my heart pounding with pride. While he was home, I would go with him to training missions wearing my small camouflage uniform, and we would drive around in his Humvee, and everyone would salute him. My dad was my hero.

In between deployments, life felt structured. Safe. When he was home, we played sports—mostly soccer, but baseball too. He coached me whenever he could. Virginia Beach was a big soccer town, and I got good. Travel teams. Competitive tournaments. It became part of my identity. When I wasn't on the field, I was on a skateboard or surfing in the water. That was my world. Cleats. Sand. Sunburn. Freedom.

My mom was great too. She was more of a free spirit, but she took great care of us when my father was away on deployments. I do remember her drinking too much sometimes. Not raging. Not violent. Just… too much. She'd get loud. Flirty. Embarrassing in a way I didn't yet have words for. I would feel this tight, hot anger rise up in me when she drank. I think it was just me being protective. She just liked to have fun.

Still, I believed we were the perfect family.

My dad had very strict standards. His phrase was simple: more A's than B's and no C's. School didn't come easily to me. In third grade, I got a C on my report card. I was terrified to show him. I didn't want to disappoint him. I didn't want to see that look in his eyes, so I did something insane. I staged a fake robbery at my own house. I turned on all the water in the house. Opened doors. Took a framed picture off the wall and placed a knife next to it like some kind of threat. Nothing was stolen. Nothing taken. I just thought if there was chaos, if there was an emergency — maybe the report card wouldn't matter. The police came. Walked through the house and looked very confused. That night, after everything had settled down, my dad still asked for my report card. The distraction didn't work.

Looking back now, I see what that moment really was — fear of not being enough. Fear of failing the standard. A willingness, even at eight or nine years old, to manipulate reality just to avoid shame.

Around that same age, something else happened — something I buried for a long time. Some babysitters crossed lines that should never be crossed with a child. At the time, I didn't fully understand what was happening. I just felt strange and guilty. Like, somehow I had done something wrong. I carried that quietly for years.

Around eleven, I started trying to run away. I don't even know why. I would sharpen pencils like they were knives, packing them like I was heading into the wilderness to survive. I'd announce I was leaving, and my mom would say, *"That's fine, but you can't take anything. Leave it all here."* I'd stomp off dramatically into the woods anyway. One day, while wandering back there, I found an older boy's fort. It had a couch inside. It felt like an adventure. Then I lifted a couch cushion, and what I found led me down a dark path.

CHAPTER 2

The First Door

There was a Playboy magazine underneath it. I remember the exact feeling, curiosity mixed with electricity. On one of the pages, there was a website listed. I tore it out. We had dial-up internet at home. The kind that screamed and beeped before connecting. I waited until I was alone and typed the website in. That was it. At eleven years old, I fell headfirst into pornography.

Looking back, it was probably a collision of things — the babysitter abuse, the confusion, the curiosity, the need to feel powerful instead of small. Whatever the cause, it hooked me fast. There was a season where I pretended to be sick for almost two months. Faked stomach problems so I could stay home alone and watch porn while everyone else was at work or school. Eleven years old.

And then, in seventh grade, the hardest thing I had ever experienced happened. I came home from school one day and couldn't find my mom. She was always there when we got home. I went upstairs and found her in the guest room, crying.

"Mom, what's wrong?"

She looked at me and said, "Shawn, I just wanted to let you know that I'm leaving."

Leaving? I didn't understand. Leaving where? To the store?

"No, Shawn. I am moving out."

The words didn't compute. My world tilted.

I called my dad at work. He made a thirty-minute drive in ten minutes. I had never seen him move that fast. He loved my mom deeply. He tried to reason with her. But she had made up her mind. That was the first time I ever saw my dad cry. A Navy commander. War veteran. The strongest man I knew. Crying.

My mom didn't disappear completely, but she never came back home. We saw her fairly often—weekends here and there. But we lived full-time with my dad. He did the best he could, but his time was stretched thin by his responsibilities at work. Still, he never stopped trying.

Emotionally, he was wrecked. He would sit and play sad love songs on repeat. For six straight months, he made the same meal: a giant pot of pasta, goulash-style. We ate it every day. Our "salad" was lettuce with salt and pepper. No dressing. Just salt and pepper. Six months. I can still taste it.

Around that same time, my dad was nearing retirement from the Navy. My grandmother, Grammy, who lived in Pennsylvania, was getting older and starting to need assistance. She was the first person who showed me who Jesus was, not through sermons, but through service. Meals on Wheels. Church every Sunday. Always serving someone.

Every weekend during the rest of seventh grade, we drove from Virginia Beach to Pennsylvania to help take care of her. Long drives. Quiet cars. A family already split, now stretched across states.

When my dad officially retired, we moved to King of Prussia, right outside Philadelphia. New state. New school. New life. My childhood in Virginia Beach ended there.

And I didn't realize it yet, but the foundation under my feet had already started to crack.

CHAPTER 3

Serf

When we moved from Virginia Beach to Pennsylvania, most people would assume it must have been difficult. For me, it wasn't. I was excited. It felt like a reset, like whatever tension had been hanging over our family might finally loosen its grip.

I watched my dad closely during that season. Even as a kid, I could see the weight he carried. Moving back to where he grew up felt important to him, and because it mattered to him, it mattered to me. We moved into the very house he had grown up in. The same hardwood floors. The same short staircase. The same neighborhood streets where he had ridden his bike and played as a kid. When neighbors saw me, they smiled and said, "You must be Serf's boy." Before long, they stopped using my full name altogether. They just called me what they had always called him — Serf.

The nickname stuck instantly. I liked the way it sounded. It felt like stepping into something already established, like walking into an identity that had history and respect behind it.

My grandmother downsized into a smaller home nearby because she didn't want the big house anymore. Eventually, my mom moved up too, so she could be close to us. For all the complicated history in our family, one thing I never questioned was that she loved us deeply.

My dad took a job as an NJROTC instructor in Allentown, about an hour away. He left before the sun came up most mornings and often came home long after it had set. He poured himself into those students, mentoring them, coaching them, shaping them. But that also meant something else for me. Freedom. Real freedom.

At thirteen years old, I rode my bike everywhere. I met a lot of kids at the local pool where everyone hung out, and just a street over from our house was a group of guys who quickly became my entire world—Gus, Dan, Matt, Joe, and a handful of others. We were inseparable.

We played baseball for hours. We stayed out late playing Capture the Flag under the streetlights. It felt like something straight out of a movie. The kind of childhood people wish they had.

But somewhere inside all that innocence, something shifted.

One afternoon, we walked into the woods with a little glass bubbler and a Ziploc full of weed. I remember being nervous, trying not to show it. Someone packed it. The bowl got passed around until it reached me. I took a hit and coughed harder than I expected. Everyone laughed. I laughed too, like that was the plan all along. Then it hit me. My chest felt warm. My head felt light. Colors seemed brighter. Sounds sharper. When we stepped back out of the woods into the sunlight, I suddenly felt exposed, as everyone could somehow tell. But underneath that paranoia was something stronger. Euphoria.

I didn't just like it. I loved it.

From that day forward, smoking became part of what we did. We would go into the woods, get high, and then go play sports for hours like nothing had happened. At the time, it felt harmless. Like we had discovered a secret version of life.

On the outside, everything looked promising. I was a strong soccer player and quickly made a select team. By sophomore year, I was getting invited to Division I college camps.

Coaches were talking to me. There was a path forming in front of me. But drugs slowly started taking priority. Weed turned into pills. Adderall. Hydrocodone. Whatever someone had. I liked the way they made me feel, sometimes confident, sometimes focused, sometimes just numb. And as my habits changed, so did my circle. I spent less time with the driven athletes and more time with the kids whose main goal every day was figuring out how to get high.

At home, my dad trusted me more than I deserved. Every morning, he would call my younger sister to make sure we were awake for school. She was five years younger than me, but somehow far more responsible. I walked her to school most mornings. And I hate admitting this now, but I was cruel to her. She played the violin, and for some reason, I thought that made me look uncool. I made her walk thirty yards behind me so people wouldn't associate us too closely. She never argued. She just did it.

Looking back now, that moment reveals something about who I was becoming — someone more concerned with protecting an image than protecting people.

Around fifteen, another shift happened. All my friends were constantly looking for weed. Someone always needed it. And I realized something. I had access. So I turned it into an opportunity. I started going to Norristown, and picking up small amounts, an ounce or two at a time. I would bring it home, sit in my room, and break it down into ten-dollar bags. Then I sold it to the same kids I played sports with. At the time, it felt smart. Entrepreneurial, even. I convinced myself it wasn't serious because it was "just weed."

But that was the moment the line was crossed. I wasn't just using anymore. I was supplying. And once that door opened, my risk-taking escalated quickly.

We were doing whippets on bus rides to soccer games. I was stealing my dad's car in the middle of the night and driving to Norristown to get high until sunrise. Then I would come home, shower, and go to school as if nothing had happened. I was living two lives.

Eventually, the police started bringing me home instead of booking me because they knew my dad. I can still picture the moment. The knock on the door. My dad is opening it. And the officer said, *"Sir... we've got your son again."* The disappointment in his eyes cut deeper than any punishment ever could. But even that wasn't enough to stop me.

Somewhere in the middle of all this, I was fifteen years old, dating a senior from a local Catholic school. She was beautiful, way out of my league in my mind. One night at a party in Bridgeport, we went upstairs together. It was my first time. I wish I could say it was amazing. It wasn't. My heart was racing, and it was over almost before it began. Maybe thirty seconds. The embarrassment was crushing. A few days later, when she wanted to see me again, I broke up with her instead. Running felt safer than vulnerability.

By seventeen, I had a fake ID because I looked like one of my friend's older brothers. I could get into bars and clubs without anyone questioning me. At the time, I felt invincible. But reality eventually caught up. During baseball season, my senior year, I was caught with marijuana and kicked off the team. Just like that. The consequences were no longer theoretical.

When my senior year of high school came to an end, I didn't exactly look like the kind of kid colleges were fighting over. I took the SAT and scored a 1010. Not terrible, but nowhere near what I was capable of. I had the talent, the opportunity, and a family that loved me, but I just never took it seriously. If anything, I was one of those kids that teachers probably looked at and thought, *"He's capable of more, he just doesn't apply himself.* I had traded discipline and potential for temporary highs.

It wasn't rock bottom. But the drift had begun.

CHAPTER 4

Brotherhood and the Bus

So when I got accepted into Bloomsburg University, a Division II school tucked away in central Pennsylvania, it felt like a win.

There was only one catch. Because of my grades, I wasn't accepted under the normal admission process. The university told me the only way I could attend was if I started early summer school and proved I could handle the academics. If I didn't maintain at least a 3.0 GPA during that summer session, I wouldn't be allowed to return for the fall semester. It was basically a probationary invitation.

Right after graduating high school, my dad helped move me into the dorms. We carried boxes up the stairs, sheets, clothes, a small refrigerator, posters — everything you need to make a dorm room feel like home. It was the first time in my life that I was really living on my own.

There was excitement in the air. College. Freedom. Independence. But there was also pressure. I knew if I didn't keep my grades up that summer, it would all be over before it even started.

So I actually tried. I went to class. I studied. I worked hard enough to keep my grades where they needed to be. That didn't mean I wasn't experiencing college life, though. I still went to parties. I met new people. And somewhere during that summer, I started experimenting with cocaine at parties. At first, it just felt like something people were doing — part of the environment.

Even with that creeping into my life, I still held things together for a while. I played intramural soccer and indoor soccer for the school. I went to the gym regularly. I balanced the social life just enough to keep my grades afloat. By the end of the summer, I maintained a 3.0 GPA and earned the right to return for the fall semester.

The fall semester is when things started getting crazier. The parties got bigger. The nights got longer. Cocaine started showing up more often. One night, I ended up at a fraternity house that would completely change the direction of my college experience — Beta Sigma Delta. They had a reputation on campus. Everyone knew who they were. They were known as the guys who sold drugs. At the time, I didn't see that as something negative. I thought it was cool. The guys in that house carried themselves with swagger. They looked like they ran the campus. They partied, they hustled, and somehow, they were still managing to stay in school. I was drawn to it immediately.

Eventually, they asked if I wanted to pledge the fraternity. I didn't really know what that meant fully, but I knew I liked these guys and wanted to be part of that brotherhood. So I said yes.

The pledge process lasted about twelve weeks, and it was one of the hardest things I have ever gone through. I won't go into detail out of respect for my brothers, but there was almost no sleep and hazing at a level most people wouldn't make it through. But the strange thing about suffering like that together is that it creates a bond. Even today, I still talk to some of those guys and respect every one of them for making it through those twelve weeks with me.

Despite the exhaustion, the fraternity made sure we still went to class. There were mornings I had barely slept, sitting in class fighting to stay awake, sometimes falling asleep at my desk. But Bloomsburg had a reputation for fraternity life, and professors often knew what pledges were going through. Strangely, I wore it like a badge of honor.

Then the spring semester came, and that's when everything really started to spiral. Now that I was a full brother, the partying ramped up even more. I was doing a lot of cocaine, and people on campus started realizing that if they wanted it, they could come to me. Eventually, the guy I was getting it from got tired of me coming back constantly. One day, he handed me a "pack" — about 50 baggies worth around $2,500. *"Bring me back $2,000,"* he said. *"You keep $500."*

I hesitated, but he made it clear this wasn't optional. The guy was intimidating, about 6'3", 300 pounds, built like a defensive end from Center City Philadelphia. Nobody on campus wanted problems with him. Just like that, I was selling cocaine.

Sometimes I would hustle hard and get caught back up on the money I owed him, but most of the time I was behind from using too much. He kept fronting me more because that was the only way I could pay him back. It became a cycle I couldn't escape.

Selling cocaine on a party school campus came with a lot of notoriety, and I liked the reputation that it came with. The benefits included free private entrances into parties, tons of new "friends," and different girls almost every night. I knew none of it was about me, it was what I had to offer. But I didn't care. I liked the attention.

Around that same time, some fraternity friends wanted weed, so we borrowed someone's mom's Nissan Sentra and drove to Philadelphia, where I picked up a pound of hydro for them. Halfway back to Bloomsburg, the engine overheated and blew up. We were stranded on the side of the highway with a pound of weed hidden in the back waistband of my friend's sweatpants.

A state trooper pulled up behind us. He separated us and started patting everyone down. When he found the weed, cop cars arrived and took my friends away one by one. I was the last one left, expecting to be arrested. Instead, the trooper looked at me and said, *"You didn't know what was going on. They just used you to drive."*

I knew that wasn't the truth. I had organized the trip.

Then he said he was taking me home. Looking back now, I understand exactly what it was. Needless to say, I was the only white guy in the car.

But in that moment, all I could think was that the police would come back later and arrest me once my friends told them the truth. For days, I waited for the knock on the door. It never came. And instead of changing my life after that moment, I kept going deeper.

By the end of the semester, I had stopped going to class completely. My grades collapsed, and I didn't even reenroll. I was living around campus, sometimes at my apartment, sometimes sleeping on the couch at the fraternity house where people would come to buy cocaine.

Then one day, someone broke into my apartment and stole the coke I was supposed to sell. Now I owed money and had no product. I knew I had to get out.

So I called my mom and told her I needed to leave. By that time, she had moved to Texas with my sister. She told me I could come, but she wasn't buying a plane ticket. *"If you want to come,"* she said, *"get on a Greyhound bus."*

So I did.

That bus ride took five days and opened my eyes to a world I had never seen before. Some of the cities and bus stations we passed through were rough. I saw drugs, prostitution, and chaos in ways most 19-year-olds never experience. By the time the bus finally arrived in Texas, I felt like I had traveled through a completely different side of America.

My mom picked me up at the station. Stepping off that bus, I thought one thing: *This is a fresh start. A new life.* I told myself I was ready to do things differently.

But the truth is… that's not exactly what happened.

CHAPTER 5

The Lake

She took me out to the lake where she and my sister were living. Their house sat right on the water, beautiful and peaceful, the kind of place that felt like a fresh start. The lake stretched out wide behind the house, and from the back dock, you could see boats cutting across the water and hear music drifting across from different parts of the shoreline. For the first time in a long time, life looked promising.

Not long after arriving, I got a job at a place called Kelly's. Around that lake, there were several bars and restaurants, and this guy named Kelly had bought up most of them. Within just a couple of days of being there, I met him, and he offered me a job. It didn't matter that I was new in town. He just handed me an opportunity.

I did a little bit of everything there. Some nights I waited tables. Other nights I bar-backed. If something needed fixing or building, I helped with that, too. One of the restaurants Kelly had purchased was floating out on the lake itself. It sat right on the water, and people could boat right up to it. I even helped with construction on that floating restaurant as they were getting it ready.

The best part of the job was how I got there. My mom's house had a dock, and sitting on that dock was her friend's jet ski. Instead of driving to work like most people, I could hop on the jet ski, fire it up, and cruise across the lake straight to the restaurant. It felt like freedom.

For a little while, it looked like I might actually be turning things around. But it didn't take long before the old version of me showed back up. Within a few weeks, I had already found the guys out on the lake who were partying. Drinking. Doing coke. Living the same kind of lifestyle I had been trying to escape. And just like that, I slipped right back into it.

My days became a cycle. Work, party, sleep, repeat. For two or three months, that was my life. Working at the restaurant during the day and partying on the lake at night. I wasn't building anything. I was just drifting.

Eventually, my mom had enough. One day, she sat me down and said something that stuck with me. *"Shawn, you're not going to live in my house and just party while working some dead-end job."* She wasn't being cruel. She was being honest.

We talked about what I should do next, and both of us came to the same conclusion. The military. Maybe structure was what I needed. Maybe discipline could straighten me out. Maybe the Marine Corps could turn me into the man I hadn't yet figured out how to become.

So I went and found a Marine Corps recruiter. I enlisted. About three weeks later, I was on a plane headed to San Diego, California, to begin boot camp at Marine Corps Recruit Depot — MCRD San Diego.

When I landed, they loaded a group of us onto a bus. None of us really knew what we were in for. The bus pulled through the gates of the depot late at night. When the doors opened, the chaos began. Drill instructors exploded onto the bus, screaming at us. We stumbled off the bus and onto something I had only seen in movies before. The yellow footprints. They lined us up on those painted footprints while drill instructors screamed in our faces, spit flying as they barked orders. It was absolute mayhem.

I had experienced hazing before from my fraternity days, but this was something entirely different. This was the Marine Corps.

The first two months were about one thing: breaking you down. We trained constantly. Physical training. Marching. Weapons handling. Rifle drills. Endless repetition. I had shown up weighing somewhere around 240 or 250 pounds. Months of beer and partying had taken their toll. But something started happening during boot camp. I began thriving. The weight started falling off. My body got stronger. My confidence started coming back.

The drill instructors noticed that I worked hard and could lead. Before long, they moved me into a leadership role. I became a squad leader. When our platoon marched, I was up front helping lead the formation. That responsibility meant something to me. For the first time in a long time, people were looking at me as someone they could follow.

Another thing that helped keep me going was the letters.

Mail call was everything in boot camp. I would get letters from my mom. Letters from my dad. Letters from the girl I was dating at the time. Those little pieces of paper meant the world when you were exhausted, sore, and homesick.

Then one day, I received a letter that caught me completely off guard. It was from my dad. He told me that he and my stepmom were expecting a baby. Not just one baby. Twins.

At the time, my dad was already in his late forties, and I remember the first reaction that hit me when I read that letter. Devastation. My mind went to a dark place. I started wondering if maybe I had been such a screw-up that he wanted to start over. I remember thinking, *Were we not good enough? Why would you want to do this again?*

Looking back now, I know that thought process was irrational. My dad had remarried and wanted to build a family with his new wife. My stepmom is a great woman, and over time, I came to see that the twins were a blessing. Still, I pushed forward.

Toward the end of boot camp, we had rifle qualification. I shot extremely well. When it was over, I had qualified as an expert rifleman.

Then came the final test. The Crucible. It was a brutal three-day event designed to push recruits to their absolute limits. We got almost no sleep. We carried heavy packs and our rifles everywhere we went. We ran field missions, obstacle courses, and endurance challenges. By the end of it, every single one of us was completely drained.

The final moment of the Crucible was a charge up a steep hill. Mud everywhere. Boots slipping. Packs are weighing us down. Recruits were scrambling and clawing their way uphill with everything they had left. But when we reached the top, something changed. We had made it.

A few days later came graduation. My family showed up to watch. My dad and my uncle were there, both Naval Academy graduates. My mom came. My stepmom came. My girlfriend at the time was there too.

Standing there in my dress uniform as a United States Marine was one of the proudest moments of my life. Marine Corps boot camp is one of the hardest things a person can go through, and I had done it.

After graduation, we got a couple of days to relax in San Diego. Then I headed back to Fort Worth to spend time with my mom while I was on leave before the next phase of training.

Instead of staying disciplined, I made a decision that I still regret to this day. I told myself I had a few days of leave, so I could party for the first couple of days and then give myself four days to get clean before returning. For two or three days, I partied hard — including excessive alcohol and cocaine. Then a buddy of mine from Louisiana drove over, picked me up, and we made the long drive back to California together.

When we got back to base, they lined everyone up for a drug test.

In Marine Combat Training, I started thriving once again. I was performing well. I became a squad leader again. I was leading my platoon during training exercises and field missions. Other Marines were looking up to me.

Then one day, about a month into training, I heard someone yell my name. *"Serfass!"*

They told me to pack my gear and get on the bus. I knew immediately what it was about. They took me to the Marine Corps legal processing area and told me I had tested positive on the drug test. My Marine Corps career was over.

They placed me in Legal Platoon while my case was processed. Whenever the other Marines wore green camouflage, we had to wear desert khaki. When they wore desert khakis, we wore green. We were meant to stand out. It was humiliating.

I tried to fight it. I begged them to give me another chance. I even had a Lieutenant General we knew from back home write a letter asking them to reconsider. For six months, I fought to remain in the Marine Corps. In the end, I lost. They discharged me with an "Other Than Honorable" separation, listing the reason as failure to adapt to military life.

I was devastated. I was so embarrassed that I lied to people about why I got kicked out.

Eventually, they processed my discharge and sent me back to Texas. Back to where I had started. Another opportunity lost due to my addiction.

CHAPTER 6

The Dealership

Coming home after my failed attempt at the Marine Corps carried a weight that was hard to explain. It wasn't just disappointment, it was embarrassment that followed me into every conversation, every look, every question I knew people wanted to ask but didn't.

So instead of telling the truth, I filled in the gaps with stories that sounded better than reality. Anything that avoided the real reason I was back: I had once again sabotaged something good because of drugs.

My mom didn’t need a full explanation to understand what had happened. She had seen enough of my patterns to recognize another one forming. She made it clear right away that coming home didn’t mean going backward. I wasn’t going to fall back into the same habits, the same environment, or the same excuses. If I was going to stay, I needed direction.

At the time, she was working with car dealerships all across the DFW area, selling warranties. Through that, she had built relationships with owners and managers — people who understood work, structure, and accountability. One of those connections was a man named Sam, who owned a dealership called Car Stop, and his sales manager, Ray Pazana. She reached out on my behalf, and before long I found myself standing in front of them, asking for an opportunity I hadn't exactly earned — but one they were willing to give me anyway.

I still had some money saved from my time in the Marines, just enough to get a room at an Intown Suites directly across the street from the dealership. It was one of those places where you paid week by week, not because you wanted to, but because you had to. Still, it gave me something I needed — a place to start over.

Selling cars came more naturally to me than I expected. It was tax season, and people were coming in ready to buy, which gave me a chance to learn quickly and produce results just as fast. Within a couple of days, I had already sold my first car. By the end of my first month, I was leading the dealership. That same month, I made over $10,000.

For the first time in a long time, it felt like I was finally gaining traction in life. I moved out of the hotel and into a small apartment nearby, and not long after that, I bought myself a GSXR motorcycle — black with dark blue accents. It wasn't the most practical decision, especially since it became my only mode of transportation, but at the time, it felt like a reward, like proof that I was moving forward.

For a short season, everything felt aligned.

One night, a guy I had sold a car to invited me out to a club on Cooper Street in Arlington, where he worked security. I showed up on my bike, parked it near the entrance, and walked in with a confidence that hadn't been there long, but felt familiar. Inside, he had a table set aside for me, and as I settled in, my attention kept getting pulled in one direction.

Across the room was a girl who stood out without trying. She had dark hair, dark eyes, and a presence that commanded attention. We made eye contact more than once, each time just long enough to acknowledge it before looking away. The only complication was that she wasn’t alone. There was a guy with her, and while I couldn’t tell exactly what their relationship was, it was enough to keep things unspoken. That silent exchange went on for hours until the moment she got up to leave.

Instead of walking past me, she came straight over, wrapped her arms around me like we were reconnecting after years apart, and casually said she hadn't seen me in so long. As she pulled away, she slipped her phone number into my hand and walked out just as smoothly as she had approached. I stood there for a moment trying to process what had just happened, knowing I had never seen her before, but also knowing I was going to reach out.

The next day I did. She agreed to come see me at the dealership, but she never showed up. No call, no explanation. It wasn't until the following day that she responded, apologizing and saying she had slept all day. That should have been a warning sign, but I chose not to see it that way.

We made plans again and met for lunch. When she pulled up, she carried the same effortless presence I remembered — Jordans, a clean outfit, and an edge that hinted at a life I didn't fully understand yet. That understanding came quickly.

Somewhere in the middle of our conversation, she mentioned that she was living in a hotel and then, almost as casually, explained that she was on the run from the police. When I asked what she meant, she told me she had been selling drugs since she was thirteen years old. It didn't match what I saw on the surface, but it also didn't push me away. If anything, it created a sense of familiarity. When I admitted that I had been involved in that world too, though in different ways — it seemed to close whatever distance there was between us.

After lunch, I took her to the mall. I didn't have much money left, maybe around $400 after bills, but I still felt the need to present myself a certain way. I ended up buying her a $300 pair of Jordan 3s, leaving myself with just enough to get by until my next paycheck.

Later that same day, I invited her back to my apartment. We spent some time talking, getting more comfortable with each other, and somewhere in that conversation, I made a decision that didn't make sense logically but felt natural in the moment. I asked her to move in. It was impulsive and reckless, especially considering everything she had just told me about her situation, but she said yes, and just like that, she was living with me.

That decision marked the beginning of a shift I didn't fully understand at the time.

That night, she introduced me to what she used — methamphetamine. When she asked if I had ever done it before, I told her I had. That wasn't true, but I wanted to seem like I understood her world. The reality was that I hadn't tried it yet, even though I had seen it before through a coworker who had left a pipe in my apartment.

That night was my first experience with it, and it didn't take long to feel how powerful it was. Sleep disappeared almost immediately. Days blurred together. My focus shifted completely. Work became less important, then irrelevant, and eventually I stopped going altogether. What had started as momentum quickly turned into neglect, and then into complete detachment.

As my routine changed, so did my thinking. I became paranoid, creating scenarios in my head about what was happening when I wasn't around. The drug didn't just affect my energy, it affected the way I processed everything. I lost weight quickly, then leveled out, but by that point, the damage was already happening in ways I couldn't fully see.

Eventually, I lost my job at the dealership. By then, I didn't care. Instead, I stepped fully into her world. Because she had a warrant out for her arrest, I convinced myself that what I was doing was helping her. I started handling everything that required being out in public. When people called, I answered. When they needed something, I delivered it. I spent my days riding all over the DFW area on my motorcycle, meeting people, making transactions, and bringing everything back.

The money came fast. Faster than anything I had ever experienced before. We were stacking cash consistently, and for a while, it felt like control — even though it was the opposite.

She was disciplined in how she operated, only dealing with people she trusted and maximizing everything she moved. I, on the other hand, began to loosen those boundaries.

At the same time, I found myself wanting something more stable with her.

CHAPTER 7

The Spiral

Despite everything, I cared about her and wanted a version of life that felt real. I convinced her to try to fix her situation by contacting her probation officer. To show her how serious I was, I proposed, and we bought rings together. The next day, I drove her to the probation office, expecting that we were taking a step toward something better. Instead, within minutes of going inside, she called me to tell me that she was being arrested. I wasn't prepared for that outcome. I didn't understand how the system worked, and I blamed myself for putting her in that position.

At the same time, I was left alone with everything she had built. All the connections, all the customers, all the responsibility. And that's where things began to spiral even faster.

Without her structure, I started making reckless decisions. I began serving anyone who reached out, regardless of who they were or how I met them. It became less about business and more about how it made me feel, important, needed, in control.

Mallory ended up in a program in Burnet, Texas, several hours away. Throughout that time, I made it a point to drive her mom there every Saturday. No matter how little I had slept or how exhausted I was, I didn't miss those trips. There were times I started drifting off behind the wheel, only to be pulled back by her mom waking me up. Looking back, it was dangerous in more ways than one.

As my visibility increased, so did the risk. I had become too open about where I lived, letting too many people into my space, mixing business with everything else. Eventually, it caught up to me.

One day, while I was out, someone broke into my apartment. They kicked the door in and took whatever they could carry, dozens of pairs of Jordans I had collected, along with a five-gallon water container filled with cash. Any bill smaller than a twenty, I crumpled up and stuffed into that jug. There had to be thousands of dollars in it.

Thankfully, our safe was bolted to the floor, and most of the money and product weren't taken. What stood out the most was what they didn't take. There were drugs sitting in plain sight, untouched. This left me confused about who would have done this, and for the first time, I started to realize that the life I thought I was controlling had already taken control of me.

I called the police because I had renters' insurance and wanted to be reimbursed for the laptop and other small things like watches and shoes that were stolen. For insurance to replace those items, I needed a police report. It was awkward to invite the police into my home with what I had going on. The officer was clearly suspicious, but he filed the report regardless. Some of my things were eventually replaced.

Even during the time Mallory was gone, when my life was completely out of control, there was always a part of me that believed

I was going to stop. I would tell myself constantly, this was the last time. Every time I re-upped, every time I picked up more, I convinced myself it was the final run. I believed it too. It wasn't like I was lying just to feel better. In my mind, I really thought I was about to turn the corner. But I never did.

Weeks turned into months, and that same promise kept repeating itself. I couldn't make it stick.

There was still something in me that wanted a normal life, though. I didn't want to be stuck in that world forever, especially knowing Mallory was eventually coming home. So I tried to create some sense of stability. I picked up a couple of jobs during that time, hoping it would give me a way out. I worked at Santander doing collections on car loans, and later, I got another job through my friend Bryan at a place called Think Cash. That was the job I had when Mallory finally came home.

I made attempts to get clean. I really did. I would stop for a couple of days at a time, trying to reset, trying to prove to myself that I still had control. But it never lasted. Something would always pull me back.

When the time finally came, I drove out to Odessa to pick Mallory up after she had spent time in a halfway house. The drive back felt like it was supposed to be the beginning of something new, but when we got back together, it was clear things weren't the same. There was a distance between us. She had been clean for a long time, and she wasn't naive. She knew I hadn't been living the same way. Even without saying it directly, she could see it in me.

We tried to reconnect, to find our rhythm again, but there was tension underneath everything. We both wanted it to work, though. That part was real. We were trying to build a life while standing on a foundation that wasn't stable. She was on parole, and I was still living between two worlds — working during the day, slipping back into old habits when no one was looking.

It didn't take long before everything got more complicated. After a couple of months, we found out she was pregnant. At first, it was a shock. It forced everything into perspective in a way nothing else had. But after that initial moment, we made a decision — we were going to figure it out.

We went and got married at the Justice of the Peace. It wasn't elaborate, but it meant something to us. We wanted to do things the right way, especially with a child on the way. Through my job, we were able to get her covered on my health insurance, which was something we knew we needed with a baby on the way. On the outside, it looked like we were stepping into responsibility.

But on the inside, I was still fighting a battle I wasn't winning. I was still using. Still selling, just on a smaller scale. I told myself I was keeping it separate, keeping it hidden so it wouldn't affect her. In my mind, I thought I was protecting her. The truth was, she already knew.

That gap between what I was pretending to be and who I was started to create distance between us. There was tension, resentment, confusion — things that don't always show up all at once but build quietly over time.

CHAPTER 8

Kaden

Looking back, one of the hardest things for me to admit is how I handled that season. While she was pregnant, I wasn't the husband I should have been. There were times I would leave her at home just so I could go get high. I told myself I was doing it so I wouldn't be around her while I was using, as if that somehow made it better. I believed I was protecting her. In reality, I was just leaving her alone when she needed me the most. That's something I still regret.

She carried our son while I was physically present at times, but not really there in the way that mattered.

On April 28th, 2010, everything changed. Kaden was born. I remember being at Baylor Hospital when it happened. Even now, that moment stands out in a way that's hard to fully explain. As much as I wish I could say I was completely present, the truth is I was still in and out, even that day, stepping outside to meet people in the parking lot, still tied to the life I hadn't let go of.

But when it came time for him to be born, everything else faded for a moment. There were complications. The umbilical cord was wrapped around his neck, and they rushed Mallory in for an emergency C-section. I was suited up and brought into the room, standing there as everything moved quickly around me. At first, they tried to deliver him through a smaller incision, but it wasn't enough. They had to open her up further, and I remember looking over and seeing more than I ever expected to see. It was intense, overwhelming, and real in a way that nothing else had been.

Then I saw him. I saw them pull him out, heard him cry, and watched them clean him off. In that moment, there was no question in my mind — God was real. There was no other way to explain what I was witnessing. Life entering the world like that, in all its rawness and intensity, changes something in you whether you're ready for it or not.

After a few days, we brought him home. I remember that first car ride vividly. I drove slower than I ever had before, completely aware of every movement, every turn. It was like everything suddenly mattered more.

We had just moved into a brand-new townhouse in White Settlement on Clifford Street. We had his room set up, everything ready for him. For a short time, we tried to live the way we were supposed to.

But I still wasn't fully there. I was still trying to live two lives, still trying to be something I wasn't ready to become.

Eventually, things started to slip again. Mallory relapsed. It's hard to even say that without taking responsibility, because the environment she came back into wasn't clean. I hadn't created a space where she could truly stay away from it. Being around me, being around that lifestyle — it caught up to her. We started using it together.

Even saying that now doesn't sit right, especially knowing we had a newborn in the house. We would use downstairs, try to clean ourselves up, and then go back to being parents. And while it may sound contradictory, we were still taking care of Kaden. She was a good mother. She was present with him, and we made sure he had what he needed. But that doesn't make it right. It wasn't the life we should have been giving him, and it's something we both still carry regret for.

Things took a turn when her C-section incision became infected. We had to take her back to the hospital to get it treated. As part of that, they ran blood work, and that's when everything came to the surface. There were traces of meth in her system. That triggered everything. They called CPS. They tested her, she failed. Then they called me in, and I didn't realize what was happening until it was too late. They gave me a mouth swab, and I failed, too.

In that moment, everything came crashing down. We weren't allowed to take Kaden home. Just like that, he was gone. He went to stay with Mallory's mom, Linda—an incredible woman who selflessly stepped in when we couldn't. That decision, as painful as it was, gave him safety during a time when we couldn't provide it the way we should have.

Around that same time, Mallory failed a drug test through parole. After trying to fight it for a short period, she was sent back to prison.

And just like that, everything I had been trying to hold together completely fell apart.

That was the point where things didn't just feel out of control, they actually were. And from there, my life started to spiral even faster than it had before.

You would think the birth of my son, and my wife going back to prison — would have been the wake-up call I needed to finally get my life together. But it wasn't. If anything, it pushed me further in the opposite direction. With my son now living with my mother-in-law, something inside of me didn't rise to the occasion — it checked out. Instead of stepping up as a father, I buried myself even deeper into the only things I thought I knew how to do: addiction and the hustle.

I tried to hold onto normal life for a little while. I kept my job as long as I could, mainly because I knew how important the insurance was. That was one of the last threads of responsibility I was still holding onto. But it didn't last long. Once my son was born, I slowly stopped showing up. First mentally, then physically. Excuses turned into missed days, and missed days turned into me just not going at all. And just like that, the job was gone.

With no structure left, everything else escalated quickly. My drug dealing didn't just pick up, it multiplied. What used to be something on the side became my entire life. My time, my focus, my energy — everything revolved around it.

At one point, I had three different houses at the same time. We still had the house in White Settlement, which was supposed to represent a new beginning. Then I got an apartment right next to my mother-in-law's house so I could stay close to my son, or at least that's what I told myself. And then there was a third place. Another apartment down the street. That one wasn't for living. That was the trap house. I never stayed there. Never slept there. It was just a place to conduct business, people coming and going, quick transactions, cash moving. It was purely functional.

Looking back, it's hard to believe how normal that all felt at the time. Three places. Three versions of my life. The one who looked like a family man. The one who tried to stay close to being a father. And the one that was fully immersed in the streets. I convinced myself I could manage all of it. But the truth was, I wasn't building anything — I was dividing myself.

Around that same time, an opportunity came that took everything to another level. There was a drought of methamphetamine in Louisiana. People I knew down there were paying around $2,800 an ounce, while I was getting it for about $800. It didn't take much thinking to realize what that meant. So I started making runs. What began as occasional trips quickly turned into almost every other day, driving from Texas to Louisiana and back, repeatedly. I was moving larger quantities and making more money than I had ever seen in my life. At the time, it felt like I had figured everything out.

But while the money was increasing, everything else in my life was falling apart just as fast. I spent more time in places I had no business being — strip clubs, back rooms, late nights that blurred into mornings. Those places weren't just for entertainment anymore; they became part of how I operated. I would sit for hours, sometimes entire days, just waiting for my phone to ring. Waiting for the next deal.

The next move. Everything revolved around that phone. Sleep became almost nonexistent. I would stay up for days at a time, running on adrenaline and poor decisions, convincing myself I was sharp and in control.

As things grew, I needed a new connection — someone who could supply the volume I was now moving. And I found one. At the time, it felt like I had leveled up. What I didn't understand was that the risks and consequences level up too.

After a few months of living like this, I convinced myself I had a plan. I told myself I would just keep going until I got caught. And when that happened, I believed it wouldn't be that bad. I had seen plenty of people get caught and walk away with probation. So in my mind, it made sense. I would make as much money as possible, and when it finally caught up to me, I would deal with it then. It was an illusion I believed fully.

Until one day, everything slowed down.

I had just left my supplier's place when I made a stop to meet someone I knew from Louisiana. We met in the bathroom, and I moved most of what I had. It was one of those moments that, looking back now, I'm probably lucky I met him when I did. By the time I left, I only had a small personal amount left — and a large amount of cash.

I got on the highway, and almost immediately, I saw flashing lights behind me. Two police cars. At first, I thought they were just passing through, so I moved over. But they didn't pass. They stayed behind me. They were pulling me over.

I exited off Highway 30 in Fort Worth and pulled into a church parking lot. I rolled down my window, trying to stay calm and act normal. Within seconds, everything escalated. They ripped my door open, pulled me out of the truck, and started yelling. They knew something. They kept asking where the drugs were, and I kept denying everything.

They searched my Tahoe thoroughly. It wasn't exactly a discreet vehicle, two-tone paint, big rims, and loud system— but somehow, I had convinced myself that it made me less suspicious. Hidden inside was a stash compartment built under the console. They couldn't find it at first. But they did find the cash, nearly $20,000. That immediately raised questions. I tried to explain it away, said it was for my wife's attorney, said I installed car stereos — but they weren't buying it.

Eventually, they called in a K9. The dog hit the console directly. They grabbed a crowbar, pried it open, and found 14 grams. Enough.

As I sat there in handcuffs, I thought it was over. This was the moment I had planned for.

But then something unexpected happened. They uncuffed me. Handed me a business card. Told me to call the number the next day. And then they let me go.

I drove home in disbelief, thanking God, convinced I had just been given a second chance. Somewhere along the way, I threw that card out the window. I never called.

And from that day on, I stopped selling drugs.

The next day, I got a job as a valet parking at the Embassy Suites in downtown Fort Worth and started trying to rebuild my life. I took the classes required to get custody of my son back and was far more present with him, now realizing I had been taking that for granted.

But deep down, there was still an unsettled feeling—like something wasn't finished yet. I just chose to ignore it, because as far as I was concerned, I had gotten away with it.

I was free. Boy, was I wrong.

CHAPTER 9

The Federal System

That uneasy feeling ended up being right. My legal problems weren't over yet, they were just getting started.

As I described in the prologue, one random December morning in 2010, my front door came crashing in. Eight to ten DEA agents flooded into my house with guns drawn. They tore my place apart, but found no drugs, no stacks of cash, just a legally owned firearm. And it didn't matter. They took me in.

That night, I was in Tarrant County Jail. Filthy conditions. Cockroaches crawling across the floor and the smell of men who had given up and hadn't showered in weeks. And that's when it hit me—this was real.

The next morning, I was unexpectedly granted bond to go home because this was my first arrest and they didn't feel I was a flight risk. I walked out knowing I didn't deserve that kind of mercy.

I honestly didn't know what kind of trouble I was in. I spent hours researching, hoping for probation but not understanding how federal cases worked. I was assigned a public defender, and with my luck, he had never handled a federal case before. I stayed with him, not out of confidence, but because I didn't know what else to do.

He advised me to meet with the DEA agents. That's when I realized, everyone had already told on me. They knew everything. I didn't give them anything new, but I owned what was mine.

At my arraignment, I pleaded not guilty — not because I was innocent, but to buy time.

During this time, I stopped using drugs, but I didn't get healthy. I was drinking a lot and eating nonstop after coming off meth for so long. I fell into depression and gained a lot of weight. I was living in fear of what was coming.

Then Mallory got out of her short prison stint and came home. For a moment, it felt like we could breathe again. But a week later, I went back to court, and my attorney told me to plead guilty. I thought I would go home after, at least until sentencing. But I was wrong.

"Your Honor, I plead guilty."

And just like that, the U.S. Marshals cuffed me.

My mind struggled to catch up with reality. One second I was standing in a courtroom, and the next I was in custody. I turned around and Mallory stood there with tears streaming down her face, and my mom stood beside her, just as broken, just as overwhelmed. It was one of those moments where words simply do not exist, only emotion, hopelessness. I didn't say anything because I couldn't. I just looked at them, trying to hold onto that image for as long as I could, knowing deep down that everything from this point forward was about to be completely different.

They didn't walk me out through the front of the courtroom. Instead, they escorted me through a back door, away from everything familiar and the life I had known. There was no ceremony to it, no pause, and no moment to collect myself. It was immediate, final, and absolute.

Outside, a transport van was waiting. It was the kind of vehicle you would never notice under normal circumstances, but from the inside, it felt entirely different. They opened the back doors, revealing a small metal cage that was barely big enough to sit in comfortably. Without saying a word, they placed me inside and locked the door behind me. There was no explanation, no conversation — just the heavy sound of the door shutting and the unmistakable click of the lock.

At that moment, I had no idea where they were taking me. The ride only lasted about fifteen to twenty minutes, but it felt much longer. Time has a way of stretching when your entire life has just been flipped upside down. Every thought grows louder. Every second feels heavier. I sat there in silence, trying to make sense of what had just happened, but there was no making sense of it. There was only acceptance, and I wasn't there yet.

Eventually, the van came to a stop. We had arrived at the federal facility in Fort Worth.

They escorted me inside and into processing, where I sat for what felt like hours. That was one of the first lessons prison teaches you, no one is in a hurry. There is nowhere to go and nothing to do but wait. Time slows down in a way that you don't understand until you're in it.

I was nervous, completely out of my element. I had never been in a real prison before. This wasn't county jail. This wasn't temporary. This was real.

They took everything from me. My clothes were confiscated, folded into a box, labeled, and prepared to be mailed back home. Every piece of normal life, every symbol of who I had been, was gone in an instant.

In exchange, they handed me an orange jumpsuit and a pair of thin, cheap, slip-on shoes that looked like off-brand Vans. They felt flimsy and uncomfortable, like they didn't belong on my feet. Nothing about them felt stable, which made sense, because nothing in my life felt stable anymore.

They also handed me a handbook and told me it would explain how everything worked. I sat there reading it while I waited, hoping it would give me some clarity, some kind of understanding of what my life was about to look like. But instead, it only made things more confusing. It was filled with rules, policies, and procedures that felt disconnected from what I was experiencing. Now I know, there is no handbook that can prepare you for prison.

Eventually, they called my name. I stood up and followed them. As we walked upstairs, the sounds hit me immediately. Keys clanged against metal doors, doors slammed shut with force, and echoes bounced through the hallways. It was constant, loud, and impossible to ignore. The deeper we went into that building, the more real everything became.

They stopped in front of a large door. When it opened, it let out a long, dragging screech that echoed through the hallway. On the other side of that door was my new reality.

The unit was one large open room. In the center sat what they called the day room, rows of metal tables bolted to the ground, surrounded by televisions mounted high on the walls. The screens were on, but there was no sound. If you wanted to hear anything, you had to buy a small radio from the commissary and tune it to the station that matched the TV. Commissary only came once a week, so for now, everything felt silent, even with all the noise around me.

Along the walls, on both the first and second levels, were rows of two-man cells stacked all the way around the room. Each cell was identical, two metal bunks, a toilet, and a sink. That was it. The "bed" wasn't really a bed at all. It was a metal slab bolted to the wall with a thin mat laid on top, about the thickness of a yoga mat. That was where I would sleep. That was home.

I stepped into my cell for a moment, looked around, and then walked back out into the unit.

And that's when I saw Cody. I had seen him before, but we weren't close. Still, he was impossible to forget. He stood around six-foot-five, close to three hundred pounds of solid muscle, covered in tattoos from head to toe. His presence alone made people nervous. He was a high-ranking member of the Aryan Brotherhood.

My heart dropped instantly. Because I already knew one thing, I wasn't joining a gang. Not a white gang, not any gang. I didn't want that life. I didn't want to owe anyone anything, and I didn't want to be told how to move, how to think, or how to survive.

But as he started walking toward me, I was scared. Not just nervous — genuinely scared.

He stopped in front of me and said, *"Hey, Shawn, let me see you in your cell really quick."*

And in that moment, every story I had ever heard about prison ran through my mind. Heart checks. Fights. Tests. I thought I knew exactly what was about to happen.

So I walked into my cell, adrenaline starting to build, preparing myself for something I didn't even know how to handle.

He reached behind his back.

And for a split second, I braced myself.

But instead of violence, he pulled out a bag of instant coffee and a small Gideon Bible. He handed them to me and said, *"These two things are all you need to make it through your whole bid. Lean into that Bible, and you'll be alright."*

In that moment, something shifted inside me. I felt God's presence in a way I never had before. It didn't make sense. The most intimidating man in the unit, the last person you would expect — was the one pointing me toward faith. But I knew one thing for certain. That moment wasn't random.

I started exercising and working out daily. It gave me structure, discipline, and something I could control when everything else felt out of control.

At the same time, I was waiting on my pre-sentence investigation — the PSI. In the federal system, they examine every part of your life, your past, your relationships, and your behavior— and build a complete picture of who you are. Then they make a recommendation for how much time you should receive, and most of the time, that recommendation is what the judge follows.

In my mind, I believed I might get three or four years. I didn't understand how the system worked yet. I didn't understand how they calculated time or how they built their case.

Then the PSI packet came.

I didn't read it all. I flipped straight to the back. They were recommending nineteen and a half years.

It felt like the ground disappeared beneath me. My stomach dropped, and for a moment, I couldn't even breathe. I couldn't process it. I couldn't accept it. And I couldn't break down in front of everyone in the unit.

So I walked to Cody's cell, the same man who had handed me the Bible when I first got there. I stepped inside, closed the door behind me, and lost it. Everything I had been holding in came out all at once, the fear, the shock, and the weight of what that number meant. He didn't judge me. He didn't look at me like I was weak. He understood. He gave me grace and helped me get my head back on straight. He explained that I could fight parts of the PSI, that I could dispute things that weren't accurate, and that it wasn't over yet.

During this time, I was focused on God, but if I'm being honest, I wasn't approaching it the right way. I was trying to bargain. I was treating God like a genie, asking Him to give me a lighter sentence, promising I would change, promising I would do better. It wasn't a real relationship yet, but even in that, God was still working on me.

I started a Bible study in a small room in the unit. I didn't care what race anyone was. I didn't care what they were in prison for. Anyone who wanted to come was welcome. It became something real. I was learning, growing, and building a foundation I had never had before. There were guys in there who really knew the Word, and being around them helped me understand things I had never understood.

But not everyone liked it.

One day, a guy from another white gang called Aryan Circle mocked it, asking if I was going to my little Bible study with all my weirdos. Without thinking, I responded the way I used to. I called him something I shouldn't have, a bitch. And in prison, that word has consequences.

Immediately, they told me to go to my cell. I wasn't ready, but it didn't matter.

I walked in, and he was already there waiting. The door shut behind me, and he threw a punch. I ducked it, grabbed him, and put him in a headlock. I dropped back and controlled him, tightening the hold but not trying to hurt him. I kept saying, *"I don't want to fight you."*

I was in full control of the situation, but then his brothers came in and started kicking me in the back of the head to get me off him.

That was the only fight I got into the entire time I was in prison. And after that, something changed. No one told. No punishment came. And they never messed with me again.

Eventually, the day came for sentencing.

The night before, I barely slept. I lay there on that thin mat, staring up at the cold metal above me, my mind racing through every possible outcome. I kept praying, trying to bargain, trying to hold onto some sense of control. But deep down, I knew I wasn't in control anymore.

The next morning, they came and got me. Back into the van. Back into the cage. Back to court.

This time, I stood in front of Judge McBryde — known as "Hang 'Em High," the hardest judge in North Texas. My attorney and I presented our disputes to the PSI. One of the biggest issues was the gun they had tried to use to enhance my sentence. But the truth was, I wasn't a felon at the time, the gun was legal, it wasn't stolen, and it wasn't connected to any drugs or money. So they had to remove it. That alone took about five years off.

Then came the moment. The judge looked down, paused, and said, *"160 months."*

I heard it, but I couldn't fully process it. My mind struggled to understand what that number really meant. I knew it was a lot. I knew it was serious. But all I could think was that it wasn't nineteen and a half years.

It felt like a win. And at the same time, it still felt like a loss.

They didn't give me time to process it. They put me back in cuffs, walked me out, and put me back into that same van — but this time, everything felt different. The first time, I didn't know where I was going. This time, I knew exactly what I was facing.

When I got back to the unit, people asked how much time I got. Saying it out loud for the first time felt unreal.

"160 months."

Some people said it wasn't bad. But to me, it felt like eternity.

That night, lying back on that same thin mat, staring at that same metal ceiling, I wasn't the same person I had been the night before. Because now, it wasn't fear of the unknown. It was the weight of the known.

And in that moment, I realized something. I could either let that number define me, or I could decide who I was going to become during that time.

That was the shift.

I didn't have control over the years. But I still had control over who I became in them.

And with that realization, something changed inside of me. Not peace. Not yet. But direction.

Because the next step was already coming, and I was about to be transferred to my first real prison.

CHAPTER 10

Oakdale

After I was sentenced and sent back to the jail unit in Fort Worth, I knew it was only a matter of time before I pulled chain to a real prison. It wasn't a question of if anymore — it was when. Every morning, I woke up knowing that at any moment, my name could be called, and my life would shift again.

I will never forget the morning it finally happened.

"Serfass. Pack your stuff."

Immediately, everything changed.

As I gathered my belongings, I felt a mix of emotions I didn't know how to process. There was fear about what was coming next, but there was also a strange sense of hope. The pretrial unit I had been in was suffocating. There was no rec yard, no library, no movement — just a constant feeling of being trapped in a box. As crazy as it sounds, I was looking forward to a real prison. At least there, I would be able to move, to build a routine, to do something with my time.

They don't tell you where you're going for security reasons. So I said goodbye to the people I had built relationships with, got on a bus, and was transported to an inmate transfer facility in Oklahoma.

While there, I met a guard who quietly told me where I was headed — Oakdale. I said, *"California?"* confusing it with Oakland, and he laughed and said, *"No, Louisiana."* I had never heard of it. My heart sank knowing I was being sent farther away from home, but I had no choice.

From Oklahoma, I was flown on what inmates call "Con Air." Rumor had it that the plane had been confiscated from George Jung, the same one featured in the movie *Blow*. It was old and even had duct tape on the wings, it didn't feel safe. Shackled to another man, walking out onto a runway, boarding an old plane that looked like it had seen better days — it was surreal.

Eventually, we landed in Louisiana and were transported by bus through swampland that felt like a completely different world. On that bus ride, staring out the window, something clicked in my mind. I was facing thirteen and a half years, and I decided: I was not going to waste this time. I was going to grow, learn, and come out better.

When I arrived at Oakdale, I was assigned to a unit where housing was segregated by race. There were no open beds in the white rooms. That's when something unexpected happened. A group of Puerto Rican guys approached me and asked if I was one of them, I guess because of my tan, they assumed I was. When I told them I wasn't, they didn't hesitate — they offered me a place to stay. Their offer became one of the biggest blessings of my time there. They took care of each other like family. They cooked together, supported one another, and welcomed me in fully. Living with them, I learned

Spanish to the point where I became almost fluent. Over time, most people in the unit assumed I was Puerto Rican. It became a running joke, but the truth was, I felt like I belonged.

In prison, everyone must work. I chose to work in the library and became a GED teacher. It was one of the most fulfilling experiences of my life. I was teaching men in their 40s, 50s, and even 60s how to read and do basic math. For the first time, I felt like I had a real purpose.

The law library was connected to where I worked, and I spent many hours researching my case. I knew something wasn't right with my sentencing, even if I couldn't fully explain it yet.

At the same time, my relationship with God transformed. At first, I had treated God like a genie, asking for outcomes. But when I was sentenced, and nothing changed, I faced a choice — to walk away or go deeper. Despite everything, I felt a peace I had never known. It didn't make sense given my circumstances. I knew it came from God. So I decided to go all in. I attended every chapel service, every Bible study. I read the entire Bible cover to cover. I prayed constantly, especially while walking the track. For the first time in my life, I stopped looking down and started looking up — literally and spiritually. I became grateful for life in a way I never had before.

Physically, I began transforming too. I built a routine of workout daily; morning and evening. Over time, I lost weight and gained strength. Other inmates noticed the results and began asking to train with me. Soon, I had a group of about ten guys working out with me regularly. I realized I was helping people in every area, physically on the yard, mentally in the classroom, and spiritually through my faith. And the more I gave, the more fulfilled I felt.

Eventually, my relationship with Mallory began to fall apart. Missed calls, distance, and a moment where she called me by another man's name made it clear that it is over. I chose to let her go. I told her to move on with her life. It wasn't just for her, it was for me. Letting go gave me peace and allowed me to focus fully on bettering myself.

As he grew, Kaden became too much for Mallory's mom to keep up with. He was brought home by the police a couple times for wandering the neighborhood in his diaper. Linda was older and was doing the best she could but thankfully my mom stepped up and brought Kaden to live with her. I am forever grateful for her sacrifice because Kaden needed the structure and I knew he was always safe now. I had 300 minutes a month on the phone and I broke that down to ten minutes a day. I would call and talk to them almost every day. Even though I was gone physically I tried to be as present as possible for my son.

After nearly two years at Oakdale, I reached a point in my sentence that I had been quietly counting down toward—I finally dropped below ten years remaining. On paper, it might not seem like much, but in that environment, it was significant. It meant I qualified for transfer to a minimum-security facility, what they call a prison camp. It wasn't freedom by any stretch, but it was a step in the right direction.

Prison camps are a completely different from regular prisons. There are no fences, no razor wire, no walls keeping you in. If someone really wanted to, they could simply walk away. But that kind of freedom is an illusion, because the moment you leave, you are running for the rest of your life. The U.S. Marshals will hunt you down, and when they catch you, you will be sent somewhere much worse. So while it may look like you can leave, almost no one takes that risk.

When it came time for me to transfer, my family was allowed to send me one outfit. My mom sent me jeans and a hoodie—something simple because at that point, I didn't know what was in style.

Then I experienced one of the strangest moments of my entire sentence. Instead of being transported in chains, I was taken to a Greyhound bus station and placed on a bus with everyday people. No one knew where I came from or where I was going. I sat there among families and strangers, looking like I belonged, even though I carried a reality none of them could see.

That bus took me to Forrest City, Arkansas. I had hoped to get closer to home, but instead, I ended up even farther away. When I arrived, I was picked up by another inmate whose job was to drive outside the camp and handle transportation and supplies. The camp itself existed to support the larger prisons nearby, handling work like landscaping, inventory, and food service.

When I got there, the openness was overwhelming. There were no fences like I said earlier, and after a couple of years behind razor wire, that kind of space took time to adjust to.

Within a couple of months, I was blessed with the best job on the compound. I was assigned to maintain the correctional officers' private gym, located about a quarter mile away. As part of that job, I was allowed to work out there. That access elevated my workout routine. Fitness had already become a major part of my life, and now I had the tools to take it to another level. I protected that opportunity with everything I had.

My faith continued to grow as I stayed committed to Bible study and church. I also earned my associate's degree through East Arkansas Community College during my time there. I was blessed with a cellmate named Sanford, known as Doc, who had been an emergency room doctor. After seeing me train others, he told me I had a gift and offered to help me get certified. Through his guidance and encouragement, I earned multiple certifications—including Master Trainer, Nutrition Specialist, Endurance Specialist, Cancer Recovery Specialist, and Strength Training Specialist. I was building a future while still inside prison walls.

Around that same time, something from my past came back to change my sentence. Back at Oakdale, I had spent hours in the law library and discovered that I qualified for a safety valve reduction that had never been applied to my case. After filing the paperwork and waiting for years, I received a letter saying my appeal had been approved. My sentence dropped from thirteen and a half years to ten.

Then, shortly after the first reduction, a federal policy change was enacted that reduced it even further, to eight years. In an instant, my entire future changed.

With my sentence reduced, I became eligible for the Residential Drug Abuse Program and transferred to Texarkana, Texas. For the first time, I was getting closer to home. My mom had been making a six-hour drive each month to bring my son to visit me, and she had taken on full custody to care for him. Those visits were my lifeline and kept me motivated to stay on track.

When I arrived in Texarkana, I went all in on the drug program. It was intense and deeply personal, forcing me to confront parts of my past I had buried for years. Through counseling, I began to understand how early experiences shaped my behavior and decisions. The program demanded accountability and challenged the way I thought about my actions. It was one of the most transformative experiences of my life. When I graduated, I was named valedictorian. Instead of making the speech about myself, I chose to speak life into the other men in the program, highlighting something positive in each of them.

By that point, my time was nearly done. Only a few months left, and I was preparing to transition to a halfway house and begin the next chapter of my life. I was also looking forward to reconnecting with Stephanie, someone from my past in Virginia Beach who had found out I was in prison and had been coming to visit me. We would talk on the phone almost every day, she really helped me pass the time. For the first time, I wasn't just thinking about getting out. I was thinking about building a future.

The last few weeks after graduating from the drug program felt like torture. Not because of anything physical, but because time itself seemed to slow down. After more than six years in prison, knowing that freedom was right in front of me made every day feel longer than the one before it. I felt a mixture of excitement and anxiety. I was excited to get out, but at the same time, I had no idea what life on the outside was going to look like anymore. So much had changed, and I had been removed from it all for so long.

Still, I reminded myself that I had spent my entire time in prison preparing for this moment. I refused to waste that time. I approached every day as if I could be released at any moment, making sure I was ready mentally, physically, and spiritually. I had worked out consistently and was in the best shape of my life. More importantly, I had developed discipline and a mindset that I believed would carry me forward to become a positive, upstanding member of my community.

Finally, the day came. My mom mailed me another basic outfit to wear out. Nothing flashy, just the same jeans and a hoodie.

On June 10th, 2016, my mom and my son came to pick me up. That moment is something I will never forget. The first thing we did was go straight to a park. I didn't want to go anywhere enclosed. I didn't want walls or buildings. I wanted open space. But more than anything, I wanted to be with my son. He had been six months old the last time I had been able to spend real time with him outside of prison. Being there with him, running around, laughing, and just being present as his father was something I had thought about for years. That day meant everything to me.

But the reality was, I wasn't fully free yet. I still had six months left on my sentence, which meant I had to go to a halfway house. My mom drove me to a facility on Avenue J in Fort Worth run by Volunteers of America. From the moment I walked in, I knew it was not a healthy environment. People were using drugs, manipulating the system, and living in ways that could easily pull someone backward. I decided immediately that I was going to do everything right so I could get out as fast as possible.

CHAPTER 11

The Second Chance

The first step was getting a job. Within the first week, I was able to get a job as a prep cook at Oliver's Fine Cuisine in downtown Fort Worth through my cousin. It wasn't glamorous work, but I was proud of it. It was honest, and it was a step forward.

At the same time, I was pursuing my passion for fitness. My mom had been attending a gym called Fit Body Boot Camp, and she spoke to the owner, Freddie, about me. When I met him, he hired me on the spot. I was incredibly proud to be a personal trainer. I threw myself into it, passing out business cards everywhere and building a reputation for creating intense workouts. People started to recognize me, and it gave me confidence that I was on the right path.

I also found a church that became a major part of my life. My relationship with God remained a priority, and it helped keep me grounded through the transition.

Then I received devastating news that Stephanie had taken her own life after battling depression. It was heartbreaking and served as a reminder of how fragile life is.

Around that same time, I met a girl named Kristy at the gym while I was working. She was doing a hip hop dance class and I couldn't stop staring at her beautiful smile and gorgeous blue eyes. She probably thought I was a creep. Our relationship started in a simple and even awkward way, especially with me not even knowing how to properly use Facebook. I had posted on her wall, thinking I was sending her a private message. I don't think her boyfriend liked it very much but their relationship didn't last much longer anyway. It was crazy how God granted me the desires of my heart. I used to pray for a beautiful, successful, petite blonde that loves the Lord and He gave me exactly that.

Over time, we grew closer. She became part of my life, spending time with me, my son, and my mom while I was on home confinement. Eventually, she shared a vision with me about opening our own gym. At first, I laughed it off because I had nothing financially to offer. I told her I had seventeen dollars to my name and less than average credit from being incarcerated. I thought I might have scared her off, but she revealed that she had been saving money over the years and felt called to use it to build something meaningful.

Our relationship grew quickly, but we waited to have sex because we wanted God's blessing on our marriage. It had been less than six months, and we decided to tie the knot. On Christmas of that first year, my son and I proposed to her together. He had gotten her a ring from the Scholastic book fair at his school. We got married on March 26th and immediately shifted into building the gym. It required a full build-out costing around $150,000, along with franchise fees and hiring staff. It was a massive undertaking, but we were committed.

One of the biggest blessings during that time was the support of Freddie, the owner of the gym I previously worked with. He mentored me not just in business but in life, constantly encouraging me to grow in my faith and be a better husband.

To build momentum for the new gym, I began hosting free workouts in a park and promoting them on social media. The turnout grew rapidly, and we built a strong community before even opening the doors. By the time we opened, we already had enough members to cover all our overhead. It was something that could only be explained by God's favor. Within one year of being released from prison, I had regained full custody of my son, gotten married, and opened a gym. It was a transformation that didn't make sense on paper, but it was real, and it was only the beginning.

The gym took off faster than anything I could have imagined. It didn't feel real at first. I remember standing there some mornings before the first class, looking around at the space we had built from nothing and watching it fill up with people who believed in what we were doing. There was a momentum in the air that you could feel, and a big part of that energy came from Chris Davila, someone I had met in the halfway house, whose contagious energy helped shape the culture of what we were building. Bringing him on as our lead trainer felt natural, and he became a cornerstone of the gym's growth until his probation officer stepped in and forced him to leave due to both of us being felons. That moment reminded me that even when life feels like it's finally stabilizing, your past can still reach forward and disrupt your progress.

A couple of years after opening the gym, a police officer who worked out with us invited me to speak at an alternative school in Arlington. I walked into that room not knowing what to expect, but what I experienced opened the door to purpose. Thirty-three kids sat there, fully engaged, asking real questions—and at the end, when only three of them raised their hands saying they had a father figure, it broke me. Driving home, I sat in silence, overwhelmed, realizing that what I had experienced wasn't just an opportunity—it was a calling. That was the moment I knew I was meant to build something bigger than myself, something that could step into the gap these kids were living in.

At the same time, I was battling something internally — imposter syndrome. A voice that kept asking who I thought I was to run a gym or mentor kids when I had just come out of prison. But I began to understand that voice wasn't truth, it was resistance — and I decided I would not wait until I felt qualified to move forward. If God placed something on my heart, then my responsibility was to act on it.

That decision led to the creation of 2nd Chance Mentors, where I began showing up weekly at an alternative school in Mansfield, pouring into kids through life skills, financial literacy, and consistent mentorship. The program expanded beyond the classroom, meeting twice a month outside of school — once for community service and once for experiences. We served wherever there was a need and gave these kids opportunities they had never experienced before, from sporting events to outings that broadened their perspective on life. Weekly check-ins became a staple, creating consistency and presence in their lives. We now have over seventeen boys committed to changing their lives and striving for more than they ever thought possible. The mentorship would not be possible if it wasn't for the help of Garrett, Bryan, and Greg. They have stepped up and sacrificially given their time and money to help these boys see their true potential and for them I am forever grateful. I could tell you story after story about the boys in our program that were dropping out of school until we showed up and walked with them through graduating. It fills my heart to see these boys start to believe in themselves.

Through all of this, I realized I didn't need to be perfect — I just needed to be present.

As I sit here writing this now, 2nd Chance Mentors has been going strong for five years and continues to grow. I recently secured a space for an after-school program where kids can come to a safe environment, work with tutors, and have a place to belong.

I want to always be honest and transparent, and there have been challenges along the way, too. COVID hit the gym hard, disrupting everything we had built, forcing us to adapt, and showing me the importance of diversifying income. That's when my best friend Bryan introduced me to roofing. I knew nothing about it, but I trusted the process, and on my very first day, I sold a roof. That moment opened my eyes to what was possible, and over the next year and a half, I built relationships, referral networks, and developed a strong sales foundation. Eventually, that same calling to build something of my own rose up again, and I started my own roofing company, creating a culture centered on faith and family.

But through all of this, it has not been perfect. There were seasons where I slipped, drinking too much, smoking weed, making small compromises that I knew could lead me back to a place I never wanted to return to. I had to make the decision to cut those things off completely. Marriage has also required growth, learning how to communicate, work as a team, and keep God at the center. After nine years of marriage, I know that our strength comes from our shared commitment to honoring God, not from perfection.

Parenting was something else I had to figure out along the way. My son Kaden is an amazing young man now, almost 16 years old, and will start driving next month. I'm so glad I was able to get home before I missed too much, and I made sure I was present for anything and everything I could be present for.

Even recently, life reminded me how fragile things can be. A fire in the unit next door filled our gym with smoke during the busiest time of the year, forcing us to relocate quickly while dealing with a landlord who failed to follow through on restoration. That situation turned into a legal battle — another reminder that challenges never fully go away.

Through everything, I've learned that success doesn't eliminate struggle. The difference is how you respond. If you take your eyes off God and focus only on the problem, you fall into self-pity — and self-pity will lead you back into old habits. But if you stay grounded, focused, and committed to your purpose, you continue moving forward.

This journey has never been about perfection. It has been about persistence, faith, and the willingness to keep showing up no matter what comes. And that is what has carried me from where I was to where I am today.

CHAPTER 12

The Five Keys

Enough about me and my story. The reason I wrote this book was never just to tell you where I've been, it was to give you something you can actually use. Something real. Something practical. Something that, if you choose to apply it, can completely shift the direction of your life.

I don't claim to have all the answers, but I do know what has worked for me, and I've seen it work for others time and time again. What I've come to believe is that success isn't random, and it's not reserved for a select few — it's built on principles. That's why I've broken it down into what I call the five keys to success. These aren't theories or ideas I read in a book somewhere, these are lessons forged through failure, pain, growth, and ultimately transformation. And I truly believe this with everything in me, if someone takes these five keys seriously and applies them consistently, their life will change. Not overnight, not without effort, but inevitably.

So now, let's get into it.

Key number one may seem obvious to some, and maybe even uncomfortable or unfamiliar to others, but it is the foundation for everything else — and that is forming a relationship with God. I'm not talking about religion, rules, or checking a box on Sundays. I'm talking about a real, personal relationship. One that grounds you when life feels chaotic, one that gives you direction when you feel lost, and one that reminds you who you are when the world tries to tell you otherwise.

For me, this wasn't something I fully understood at first. It took brokenness, it took humility, and it took reaching a point where I realized I couldn't do life on my own anymore. But when I finally surrendered and started seeking God, not just in moments of desperation, but daily, intentionally — everything began to change. My mindset shifted. My decisions changed. My purpose became clearer.

A relationship with God gives you a compass in a world full of distractions. It gives you strength when there is no strength. It teaches you discipline, patience, forgiveness, and perspective. And most importantly, it gives you identity — not based on your past, your mistakes, or what others think about you, but based on who you were created to be. If you build your life on that foundation, everything else you pursue will have meaning, direction, and staying power.

Key number two is finding a mentor, someone who has already done what you're trying to do, someone who has walked the path you're on and understands both the shortcuts and the pitfalls along the way. A mentor isn't just there to give you advice, they help you create real, actionable goals, and more importantly, they hold you accountable to those goals when your motivation fades. Because it will fade. There will be days you don't feel like putting in the work, days you start to justify slipping back into old habits — and that's exactly where a mentor becomes invaluable. They don't let you stay comfortable, and they don't let you lie to yourself.

It is important that it must be someone you genuinely respect, someone whose life, discipline, and results you admire — because that respect creates a level of accountability that hits differently. When you respect someone, you don't want to let them down. You don't want to show up unprepared, make excuses, or waste their time. And that pressure, in a healthy way — pushes you to become better.

A mentor can condense years of mistakes into months of progress by helping you avoid what doesn't work and doubling down on what does. Instead of guessing your way through life, you're learning from experience that's already been tested. In my experience, that can be one of the fastest ways to change the trajectory of your life.

Key number three is committing to continuous self-improvement, making the decision that you are never going to stay the same, that you are always going to be growing, learning, and becoming better than you were yesterday. This isn't a one-time decision, it's a daily discipline. It shows up in how you take care of your body through exercise, because physical strength builds mental toughness and confidence. It shows up in your commitment to education, whether that's formal learning, reading books, listening to podcasts, or surrounding yourself with people who challenge you to think bigger. It shows up in self-help, in doing the internal work —

learning your patterns, facing your weaknesses, and choosing to grow instead of avoiding hard truths.

Real self-improvement is about becoming more disciplined, more aware, and more intentional in every area of your life. It's about understanding that where you are right now is not where you have to stay. When you commit to improving yourself daily, even in small ways, those small wins start to stack, and over time, they create massive change. You begin to carry yourself differently, think differently, and make better decisions. And the truth is, success isn't something you chase — it's something you grow into. When you become better, your life follows.

Key number four is what I call "show me your friends, and I'll show you your future." Who you surround yourself with is one of the biggest factors in the life you will end up living, whether you realize it or not. There's a saying that your income tends to mirror the average of the five people you spend the most time with, and from what I've seen, that holds a lot of truth. The people around you influence what you believe is normal. They shape how you think, how you speak, what you tolerate, and what you strive for. If you're constantly around people who lack ambition, who settle, who spend their time complaining or distracting themselves, it becomes incredibly hard to rise above that environment — because it starts to feel acceptable. On the other hand, when you surround yourself with people who are disciplined, driven, and focused on growth, it naturally raises your standard. You start thinking bigger, moving differently, and holding yourself to a higher level.

This doesn't mean you turn your back on people, but it does mean you have to be intentional about proximity. You have to protect your environment because your environment is shaping you every single day. If you want a different future, sometimes it starts with choosing different people to walk alongside you.

Lastly, ***key number five*** is the importance of giving back and serving others. This is one of the most powerful shifts a person can make because it takes the focus off of ourselves and places it where it belongs — on making an impact. Serving others has a way of breaking selfishness and putting life into perspective. It reminds us just how much we actually have, even in seasons where we feel like we're lacking.

So many times, we get stuck in our own heads — caught in self-pity, focused on our problems, our setbacks, and what isn't going our way. But the moment you step into someone else's struggle and become part of their solution, something changes. You realize there are people fighting battles you can't even imagine, people who would trade places with you in a heartbeat — and it creates a sense of gratitude that you can't fake.

Giving back doesn't just help others, it transforms you. It builds humility, purpose, and a deeper sense of fulfillment that money or success alone can't provide. And what's incredible is that the more you give, the more you grow. It shifts your mindset from scarcity to abundance, from *"what can I get?"* to *"what can I give?"* And when you live like that, success stops being just about you — it becomes something much bigger, something that actually matters.

As you close this book, I want you to understand something — none of this matters if you don't take action. My story isn't meant to impress you, it's meant to show you what's possible. No matter where you've been, what you've done, or how far off track you feel, your life can change. But it won't change by accident. It changes when you make a decision, when you decide to live differently, think differently, and hold yourself to a higher standard.

These five keys aren't complicated, but they are powerful if you actually apply them. Build a relationship with God, find a mentor, commit to growing every single day, be intentional about who you surround yourself with, and give back to others. If you do those things consistently, your life will not stay the same — I would bet everything on that.

So don't just walk away from this book inspired, walk away committed. Committed to becoming the person you know you're capable of being.

Your past doesn't define you. Your circumstances don't control you. And your future is still yours to build.

Now it's on you, go live it.

ABOUT AUTHOR

Shawn Serfass is a speaker, entrepreneur, mentor, and host of the *Forgiven AF* podcast, but his story did not start anywhere near where it is today.

Before the purpose, before the platform, there was a life built on bad decisions, fast money, and consequences that eventually landed him in prison. Shawn was involved in drug dealing and living a lifestyle that led to his arrest, one of the moments that forced him to come face-to-face with the reality of where his choices were taking him. What felt like control was actually destruction, and what looked like success was leading straight to a dead end.

But God had a different plan.

Through faith, accountability, and complete surrender, Shawn began rebuilding his life from the ground up. Not overnight, and not without struggle, but with a conviction that his past would no longer define him. What once was shame became purpose. What once was broken became a testimony.

Today, Shawn is the founder of **2nd Chance Fitness** and **2nd Chance Mentors**, a nonprofit dedicated to guiding at-risk youth toward a better path. Through his mentorship, speaking, and the *Forgiven AF* podcast, which reaches over a million incarcerated listeners, he shares a message rooted in truth: no one is too far gone for God to restore.

Forgiven AF is his story—unfiltered, honest, and faith-driven. It is not about being perfect. It is about being forgiven

RESOURCES

Forgiven AF Podcast

Forgiven AF features conversations with entrepreneurs, mentors, and change-makers who turned their worst decisions into their greatest purpose.

Raw, unfiltered, and real—Forgiven AF dives into stories of failure, redemption, faith, and second chances. From prison cells to purpose-driven lives, each episode proves that your past doesn't define you—your comeback does.

Listen. Watch. Share the message.

Available on all major platforms
Search: Forgiven AF Podcast

Reaching over **1 million incarcerated listeners nationwide**

Forgivenaf.com

- ✓ YouTube
- ✓ Spotify
- ✓ Apple
- ✓ Amazon

All available podcast networks

Facebook @forgivenafpodcast

IG @forgivenafpodcast

2nd Chance Mentors

2909 Turner Warnell Rd suite 151

Arlington, TX 76001

Be who you needed…

2nd Chance Mentors is a 501(c)(3) nonprofit organization dedicated to guiding at-risk youth toward a better future through mentorship, accountability, and real-life support. We work directly with students who have been removed from traditional school environments, providing consistent guidance, life skills, and a safe place to grow. Our mission is simple: meet them where they are, build trust, and help them realize their potential, no matter their past.

Facebook @2ndchancementors

2ndchancementors.org

IG @2ndchancementors

SEATGEEK

www.ingramcontent.com/pod-product-compliance
Lightning Source LLC
LaVergne TN
LVHW020513100826
845148LV00003B/770

* 9 7 9 8 8 9 5 7 1 4 0 2 7 *